BENCHMARK BIOGRAPHIES

# The Man Who Painted Indians
## GEORGE CATLIN

by Nancy Plain

**BENCHMARK BOOKS**

MARSHALL CAVENDISH
NEW YORK

Special thanks to Joyce Stanton, my editor and friend

All works of art in this book are by George Catlin.
Front cover: *Comanche Feats of Horsemanship,* 1834–35
Back cover: Self Portrait, 1824

Benchmark Books
Marshall Cavendish Corporation
99 White Plains Road
Tarrytown, New York 10591-9001

© Marshall Cavendish Corporation 1997

Library of Congress Cataloging-in-Publication Data
Plain, Nancy.
The man who painted Indians : George Catlin / by Nancy Plain.
p.    cm. — (Benchmark biographies)
Includes bibliographical references and index.
Summary: A biography of the painter, author, and ethnographer who devoted himself to recording
Indian life, not only in this country but in South America and Asia.
ISBN 0-7614-0486-4 (lib. bdg.)
1. Catlin, George, 1796–1872—Juvenile literature. 2. Painters—United States—Biography—Juvenile
literature. 3. Indians of North America—Pictorial works—Juvenile literature. [1. Catlin, George,
1796–1872. 2. Artists. 3. Indians of North America—Social life and customs.] I. Title. II. Series.
ND237.C35P57  1997      759. 13—dc20      [B]      96-5623   CIP   AC

Printed in Hong Kong

Photo Credits. Back cover: courtesy of Thomas Gilcrease Institute, Tulsa, Oklahoma. All other
photographs in this book are used by permission and through the courtesy of: National Museum
of American Art, Smithsonian Institution/Gift of Mrs. Joseph Harrison, Jr.

1   3   5   6   4   2

*For Alan, Sarah, Katherine, and Amy, with love*

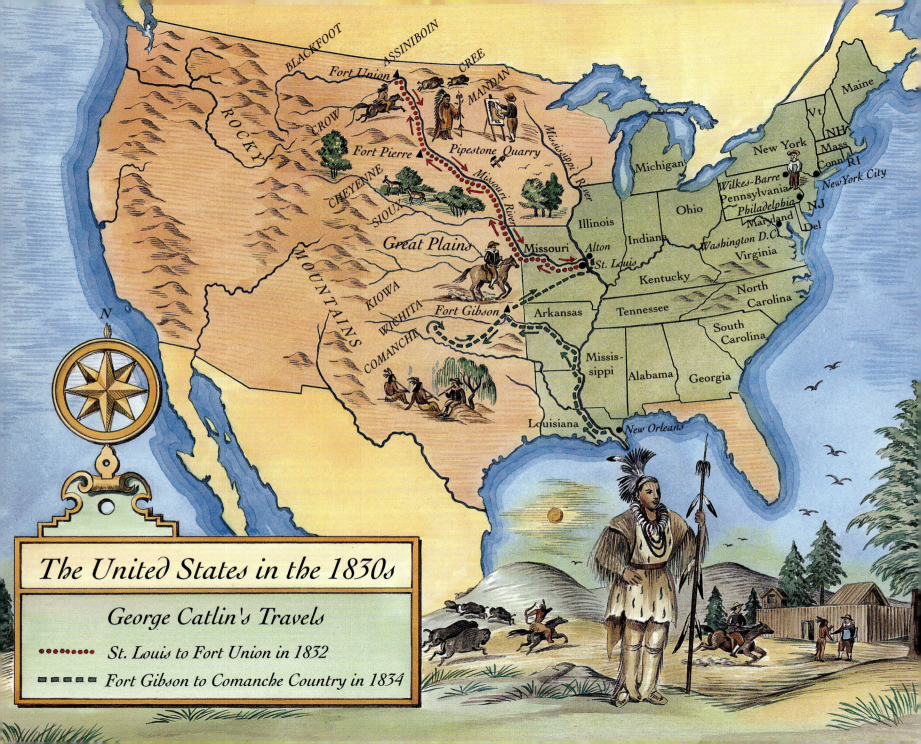

The United States in the 1830s

George Catlin's Travels

• • • • • St. Louis to Fort Union in 1832

▪ ▪ ▪ ▪ ▪ Fort Gibson to Comanche Country in 1834

# CONTENTS

*When George grew up, he roamed the West, painting pictures of Native Americans.*
*This is Chief Running Fox on his favorite horse.*

# GEORGE CATLIN, ARTIST

When George Catlin was a new-born baby, the United States was also new. It had only sixteen states, all clustered east of the river the Indians called the "Father of Waters"—the Mississippi. George's first home was in Pennsylvania, in a town called Wilkes-Barre. It was a little town with fifty houses and streets that turned to mud when it rained. The road out of Wilkes-Barre was a path made by Indians long ago. One day George would wear soft moccasins and walk on many Indian paths. And he would become a famous painter. But when he was born—on July 26, 1796—he was just the fifth baby of Putnam and Polly Catlin.

When George was four his family moved to New York State to live on a farm. It was the perfect place for him because there was always something new to see. Whenever he could, George went exploring. In the dark, whispering forest, he learned the habits of deer and squirrels and blacksnakes. He fished in the creek and dug for Indian arrowheads in the fields. Once he found a real tomahawk, without a handle.

At bedtime, by firelight and candlelight, the Catlin children—there would be fourteen in all—listened to stories of the old days. George's father, Putnam, had been a fife-and-drum boy in the American Revolution. His mother, Polly, had been captured—and freed—by Iroquois (EAR-ah-kwoy) Indians in that same war. George wondered, When would something really exciting happen to him?

## A HUNTER IN THE WOODS

One day it did. When he was ten George secretly planned to kill his first deer. When no one was looking he sneaked off to the woods carrying his big brother's man-sized rifle. Just before dark a deer

*George's mother, Polly Catlin,*
*who had been captured by the Iroquois*

wandered by, and George took aim. *Bang!* The deer fell dead. But George hadn't even pulled his trigger yet. Someone else had killed it!

Out from the woods stepped a tall Indian with long black hair. George froze. Would he be captured like his mother? Would he be scalped? He didn't move a muscle until the Indian carried the deer away. Then he raced home.

To George's surprise, his father wanted to welcome the deer hunter. Putnam knew that the land he owned had once belonged to Native Americans. But as whites had settled the eastern part of the United States, the tribes had been forced to move again and again. Now the eastern Indians had very little land left, and their lives were hard.

George and his father found the stranger camping in a field. He was an Oneida (o-NI-dah) Indian, part of the Iroquois people, and his name was The Great Warrior. He and the Catlins became friends.

The Great Warrior made new arrows out of George's old arrowheads. He made a handle for George's tomahawk and taught him how to throw it, too. When it was time to say good-bye, the Catlins were sad and worried. They were right to worry. A few days later a farmer shot and killed their friend as he headed home to his people.

**GEORGE GROWS UP**

As the years passed, George thought a lot about The Great Warrior and the Indian way of life. Like his lost friend, George was happiest when he was outdoors, with "a fishing pole in one hand and a rifle in the other." He would much rather not be in school. But cooped up in the classroom, he found another way to explore: with his pencil. He doodled on his Greek papers; he drew on his desk. He imagined paintbrushes dripping with color—dark green for the pine trees, light green for the fields.

Art was fine for a hobby, thought George's parents. But what should their son do for a living? Be a lawyer, like his father, they decided. So when George was twenty-three he began to practice law.

For George, the courtroom was a lot like school. Flies buzzed and the judge's voice made him sleepy. When he started doodling on the lawyer's table, he knew it was time to quit. He sold all his law books to buy artist's supplies, and in 1823 he moved to Philadelphia—to do what he really wanted to do.

## BECOMING AN ARTIST

The sign outside his new studio read, GEORGE CATLIN, MINIATURE PAINTER. He painted tiny portraits on three-inch pieces of ivory. He also painted large portraits that people hung over their fireplaces. Orders for pictures, big and small, came in fast.

But life was still not exciting enough for George. Even though he painted famous people, like Dolley Madison (wife of President James Madison) and DeWitt Clinton (governor of New York State). Even though he married his sweetheart, Clara Gregory. George was looking for one big idea to work on, a

*Clara, George's beloved wife*

"noble purpose" for his art.

And he found it. A group of Indians from the West passed through Philadelphia on their way to Washington, D.C. They were not poor like George's old friend The Great Warrior. Whites had not yet taken their land. Graceful and proud, they lived on the Great Plains, that sweep of country few white Americans had ever seen.

## A DARING PLAN

The Plains Indians, in their eagle feathers and buffalo robes, were the exciting subject he had been looking for. An artist could happily spend a lifetime painting their portraits, thought George. But what would happen to the Indians, he wondered, as more and more settlers pioneered across country? He decided

*Chief Black Rock, a Plains Indian,*
*wearing his eagle feathers and buffalo robe*

to go west to paint the tribes before everything changed. Before it was too late.

Everyone except his wife, Clara, thought George's plan was crazy. He might drown in a river or be clawed to death by a grizzly bear. But George had made up his mind to paint the first Americans, and that was that.

"Nothing short of the loss of my life shall prevent me from visiting their country and becoming their historian," he wrote.

He went alone to St. Louis, Missouri, where all trips west began.

# THE MEDICINE PAINTER

St. Louis, Missouri, was a frontier town on the banks of the great Mississippi River. Beyond it lay the West—a vast, mysterious wilderness with no roads. From St. Louis fur trappers and traders, pioneers and explorers headed west. Little by little, white people were pushing their way into Indian country, making their own claims on the land. In 1830, when George Catlin arrived in St. Louis, the riverfront was a jumble of big, puffing steamboats, flat-bottomed cargo boats, and slender Indian canoes.

Right away George made friends with William Clark, who had led the famous Lewis and Clark Expedition of the Northwest in 1804. Now the white-haired Clark was in charge of all government dealings with western Indians. George packed his paints, threw his sketchbook over his shoulder, and went with Clark to a treaty signing. The Indians of the Upper Mississippi were being forced to sell their land—again.

This was an old story for Indians who lived near whites. The whites made

*St. Louis, a busy town on the Missippi River*

treaties only to break them when they wanted more land. There were twenty-four states in the United States by 1830, and President Andrew Jackson, whom the Indians called "Sharp Knife," wanted more. He said that the "savages" must always move west to make way for the settlers—or die fighting. One chief who fought hard was the proud Black Hawk, who would tell President Jackson, "You are a man; I am another."

At the treaty signing George listened to angry speeches and sad speeches. He painted pictures of men from Upper Mississippi tribes—Sauk and Fox, Missouri, Omaha, Iowa, and eastern Sioux.

Yet George had come west to see the Indians who still ruled their own land. On the Great Plains that stretched westward to the Rocky Mountains, Native

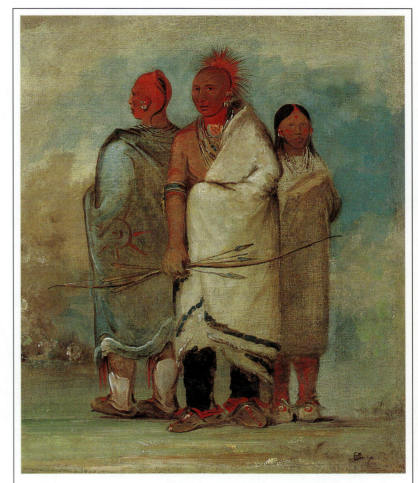

*Three people of the Sauk and Fox tribe*

Americans were hunting and traveling just as they had for centuries. It was George's dream to paint their pictures so they could never be forgotten.

**A TRIP UP THE MISSOURI RIVER**

The only path to their country was another great river—the Missouri. It was fast, twisting, and filled with sunken logs. No boat had ever steamed far up the "Big Muddy." Not until 1832.

Then a shiny new double-decker steamboat called the *Yellowstone* started upriver. Its job was to reach Fort Union, a fur-trading post two thousand miles (3,200 kilometers) to the northwest. George packed his paints, threw his sketchbook over his shoulder, and climbed aboard.

Up and up the swirling, chocolate-col-

ored Missouri chugged the *Yellowstone*. Deeper and deeper into the wild places. Indians in villages along the way called the strange, noisy boat "The Big Thunder Canoe." George sat on the top deck, painting pictures and writing in the journal that he would later turn into a book. He missed Clara, but he was happy steaming through the Great Plains.

Ducks, geese, and swans swam in the water or flocked on the shore. Grizzly bears prowled in the high bluffs that lined the river. Beyond the bluffs stretched the prairie, in places hilly and in places flat as a table. There antelope, elk, and wild horses ran free. And millions of buffalo grazed.

It was a land, George wrote, of golden sunlight and long shadows. And everywhere there was grass. It covered the

*The Missouri River flowed past beautiful bluffs and prairie*

earth like a green-velvet carpet, splashed with sunflowers and wild roses. The prairie wind rushed through the grass, never stopping.

More than one thousand miles (1,600 kilometers) above St. Louis, the steamboat became stuck in a shallow stretch of the river. So George and twenty other passengers waded to shore, put on deerskin moccasins, and hiked ahead. After two hundred miles they reached a trading post called Fort Pierre (in present-day South Dakota). This was Sioux (SUE) country, and many Sioux families were camped nearby.

## PAINTING THE SIOUX

I was luckily born in time to see these people, thought George. He quickly painted a portrait of One Horn, a great chief, whose enemies' scalplocks were sewn in a fringe on his shirt.

In shock the Sioux stared at the portrait, the first one they had ever seen. It looked alive! Were the painted eyes staring right back at them? Could those eyes close at night? The people called George "Medicine Painter" because *medicine* meant mystery and power. His art, like all medicine, must be a special gift from the Great Spirit. Such a powerful gift, they said, had to be dangerous.

But George's friendly manner convinced the Sioux that his pictures would not harm them. He also learned to "talk" to them in the sign language that all Plains Indians understood. Sketching with brown ink and painting with oils, he made pictures of women and warriors, great chiefs and tiny children. He

*Hundreds of Sioux tepees near Fort Pierre*

painted the Sioux dancing, working, hunting, and playing ball.

In just a few weeks George did what no white artist had ever done in those days before the camera: He told the story of Sioux life in pictures.

The Indians held a feast in honor of the men from the *Yellowstone*. After eating, everyone smoked the long-stemmed pipe. Chief One Horn told his guests, "We give you our hearts in this feast … and the Great Spirit will seal our friendship."

### A FIGHT IN THE CAMP

Soon, though, George's art caused a tragedy. One day he decided to paint the warrior Little Bear in profile, showing one side of his face instead of the usual full-face view. But as George worked, a

*Chief One Horn, whose picture George painted first at the Sioux camp*

jealous chief named The Dog made fun of the portrait.

"Little Bear is but half a man."

Little Bear looked up. "Who says that?"

"The Dog says it," answered the troublemaker.

"Why does The Dog say it?" asked Little Bear, in silent rage.

"Ask the Medicine Painter. He can tell you. He knows you are but half a man—he has painted but one half of your face and knows the other half is good for nothing!"

Still Little Bear held his temper.

Only when the painting was finished did the two men start to fight. The Dog shot Little Bear to death and ran from the camp. In their grief, some people blamed George Catlin for Little Bear's death.

"Both sides of his face were good, and the medicine man knew it also! Why was half of his face left out?" They began to call for George's death, too.

Luckily for George, the *Yellowstone* had finally steamed upriver and arrived at Fort Pierre. He and the other travelers hurried to the boat and escaped the next day. Sooner than they had planned, they were again heading north.

# WILD SPIRITS

The *Yellowstone* was the first steamboat ever to reach Fort Union. This was Crow and Blackfoot country, but the fort was a meeting place for other Plains tribes, too: Assiniboin (ah-SIN-ah-boyn), Ojibway (OH-jib-way), Cheyenne, and Cree.

The Indians who traded at Fort Union reminded George of knights of old. He wrote in his journal that they were the "finest looking . . . most beautifully costumed" of any Indians in the West. The Great Spirit had made them rich in land and buffalo. They were free on the Great Plains, with everything they needed for a good life.

George's studio was a gun room high up in the fort, overlooking the rolling prairie. He sat on a cannon to paint while crowds gathered to watch the magic of his art. Because many who watched were deadly enemies, they had to leave their weapons at the door. But George felt their "wild spirits" and knew that a fight could break out at any time.

He was in a hurry to "paint and scrib-

*A Crow tepee made of decorated buffalo skins*

ble" everything he saw: a Blackfoot chief and his grandson (who had twice been kidnapped by the Crows); a woman named Crystal Stone; a warrior named Eagle Ribs, who had taken the scalps of many fur traders.

### THE ROLLING PRAIRIE

Riding out on the prairie, George sketched a Crow tepee, white as a cloud. He painted White Buffalo the medicine man as he danced and prayed over a dying Blackfoot brave. The picture of this mysterious scene was one of George's favorites.

Carrying his rifle and his sketchbook, George rode with the young Indian men to hunt buffalo. On fast ponies they went "flying over the carpeted prairie."

For the Native Americans the buffalo

*The Blackfoot boy who had been kidnapped by Crows and rescued by his own tribe.*

was life. They ate its meat freshly roasted, or dried it in strips called pemmican (PEH-mih-kahn). Tepees, warm robes, and saddles were made from the hides. The people made spoons from the animals' horns, glue from the hooves, and even fly swatters from the tails. They were grateful for the buffalo and followed them everywhere.

## THE BUFFALO ARE DYING

But now fur traders were giving Indians guns, blankets, and cheap beads in exchange for great piles of buffalo hides. Worse, they were tempting the hunters to kill thousands of animals just to get whiskey.

George worried that one day there would be no more herds. White settlers would sweep across the West like a

*White Buffalo, the medicine man, wears a bearskin as he prays over a dying man.*

*A rooftop view of the Mandan village*

prairie fire, he predicted. "Whiskey and trinkets" would destroy the old ways forever.

### DOWNRIVER BY CANOE

On a summer morning George left Fort Union to return to St. Louis. This time he traveled by canoe, paddling down the Missouri River. His companions for the long journey were two fur trappers, Jean Ba'atiste and Abraham Bogard. Their canoe glided past cliffs that were shaped like tumbledown castles. At night the men camped on the riverbank.

One morning they awoke to find a mother grizzly bear and her two little cubs in their camp. From the huge paw prints George could see that the mother bear had been sniffing his toes while he slept. She had also eaten most of his supplies, including his paints!

Bogard warned George not to shoot. "These darned animals are too much for us," he said.

Quickly the men escaped to their canoe and paddled away. (Worse than grizzlies, George later joked, were the mosquitoes that were eating them alive every night!)

### MEETING THE MANDANS

George and his guides visited the friendly Mandan Indians, whose village he thought was the "strangest place in the world." These Indians lived, not in tepees, but in round log houses covered with clay. George climbed onto the dome-shaped roofs where the Mandan liked to sit. From his perch George painted scenes of the village below.

Oddly, many of the Mandan had blue eyes and light streaks in their hair. George painted a beautiful girl named Mint and a young man called The White Eyebrows.

Although he did not speak the Mandan language, George became close to a noble Mandan chief named The Four Bears. In silent friendship they gave each other gifts and feasted on buffalo ribs and wild turnip pudding.

**CEREMONY OF THE GREAT FLOOD**
Strangest of all was the Mandan religious ceremony called *O-kee-pa*. It was a celebration recalling the Great Flood of ancient times, part of Mandan legend. It was also a time for the people to pray for plentiful buffalo. For four days drums pounded and the villagers danced to make the buffalo come. And inside the sacred lodge, young men proved their bravery by undergoing self-torture. George was one of the few white men ever allowed to watch this torture. It was so severe that it made him cry.

The paintings George made of his Mandan friends are the only pictures of this tribe. A few years after George's visit, white traders would unknowingly bring smallpox to the Upper Missouri country. The terrible disease would spread to many tribes, and most of the Mandan would die.

In the autumn of 1832 George's little canoe reached St. Louis. When he looked back on his life with the Indians of the Great Plains, he wrote, "I love these people who have always made me welcome to the best they had."

*At the O-kee-pa Ceremony, the Mandans danced to make the buffalo come*

# COMANCHE COUNTRY

George spent more than a year traveling with Clara. Together they relaxed in the warmth of Florida and exhibited Indian paintings in New Orleans. Then George was ready for another adventure. The United States Army planned to explore the Southwest, and he got permission to go along. This was the land of the Kiowa and Wichita tribes and of the warlike Comanche (kah-MAN-chee). The government knew even less about the Southwest than it did about the land of the Upper Missouri. Like George's ride on the steamboat *Yellowstone*, this trip would be another historic first. Saying good-bye to Clara in New Orleans, George traveled by steamboat to Fort Gibson, where the army's expedition would begin.

Four hundred soldiers started out from the fort in June 1834. Bugles rang out gaily, and each company of men rode a different-colored horse. Near the front of the line rode George on his fast, new cream-colored mustang named Charley.

*On fast horses, Indians hunted the buffalo*

At first the men passed through green valleys and prairies. They killed buffalo for food and picked wild plums and berries along the way. The air was sweet with the scent of wildflowers.

But farther west, in the blazing heat, water was scarce. A terrible fever spread through the regiment. Men and horses began to die. Only half of the men, including George, were well enough to ride on.

Deeper into Comanche country, they spotted a war party on a distant hill. Would the Comanches attack? When the soldiers held up a white flag, the Comanche leader rode across the prairie to them, prancing and leaping on his white horse. His name was The Spaniard, and he shook hands with each soldier. In friendship, the Indians led the men to their village.

Here George made the first paintings ever of Comanche life. These people were the greatest horsemen of all. They seemed more comfortable on a horse than on their own legs. George painted them as they tamed wild stallions. He painted them as they rode at full speed, hanging sideways on their ponies while shooting arrows under the animals' necks!

## A LONG RIDE HOME

But George had caught the fever and was getting weaker every day. On the way back to Fort Gibson with the regiment, he was too sick to ride and had to be carried in a wagon.

For weeks George lay sick at the fort. He wondered if he would ever again see

*George and the soldiers meet a dashing Comanche chief*

*Pipestone Quarry, where Indians found the red stone to make their pipes*

Clara, who was waiting for him in Alton, Illinois. As soon as he was better, he mounted Charley and set out to see her. It was a long trip—five hundred miles (800 kilometers)—across the prairie. But George was not afraid to go alone. By now he was a rugged explorer. He followed his compass under the big prairie sky. At night he slept snug in his buffalo robe by the campfire, while wolves howled in the distance.

## THE SACRED QUARRY

Two years later George headed west for the last time. With his friend Robert Wood, he set out to see the Pipestone Quarry, in present-day Minnesota. There Native Americans from almost every tribe found the red, claylike stone that they used to make their peace pipes.

The Great Spirit had made the quarry sacred ground, though, and whites were not welcome. Angry Sioux tried to stop George and Robert on their journey.

"We know that the whites are a great cloud that rises in the East and will cover the whole country.... No white man has ever been to the red pipe and none shall go!"

As always, George was too curious to turn back. He told the Indians that he meant no harm. Besides, he said, "We have started to go and see it, and we will not be stopped."

The Sioux finally allowed the men to visit the ancient place. George collected a sample of the red stone, which to this day carries his name: "Catlinite."

# THE INDIAN GALLERY

Now George had completed the first part of his dream. During six years of travel in the West, he had made a record in pictures and writing of the Plains Indian way of life. No one had ever done this before. And no one would ever do it in the same way again, because the Indians' world would soon be changed forever.

George came out of the wilderness with five hundred paintings and many objects—beautiful clothes, weapons, jewelry, drums, peace pipes, and even a Crow tepee. He called his collection "Catlin's Indian Gallery." The second part of his dream was to show his Gallery to the world.

## TELLING THE INDIANS' STORY

His first large exhibition—in New York City—made him famous. New Yorkers waited on long lines to see it. George held up his paintings and talked about the people in them. Some in the audience called him a genius. But some thought he must be lying, especially

*George compares the sizes of a grizzly bear and a mouse*

when he described the frightening Mandan torture ceremony, *O-kee-pa*. People also wondered how one man could have seen and done so much.

Chief Running Fox, of the Sauk and Fox tribe, visited the show with some of his tribesmen. When his companions saw George's picture of Running Fox on horseback, they jumped out of their seats, shouting with amazement.

Running Fox said to the audience, "My friends, I hope you will pardon my men for making so much noise, as they were very much excited by seeing me on my favorite war horse."

George closed the New York show in December 1837 when his first child, Elizabeth, was born. Four months later he moved the Gallery to Washington, D.C. He hoped that Congress would buy

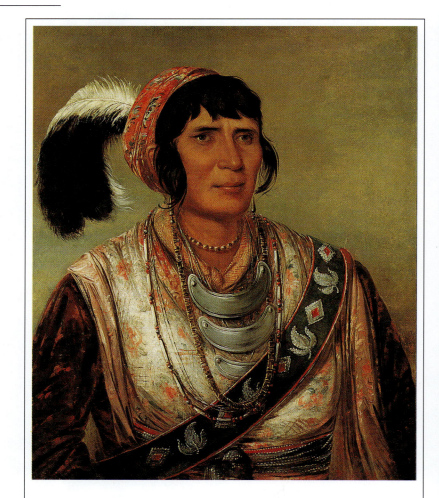

*Osceola, a great Seminole leader, fought to keep his nation's Florida homeland. This was one of the most popular pictures in the Indian Gallery.*

his collection and display it in a special national museum.

But at the exhibit he talked about how fur traders were bringing whiskey and smallpox to the Great Plains. He called for the government to stop taking Indian lands. Some senators agreed with George, but most did not. Many were angry at his support of the Indians, and they prevented Congress from discussing purchase of the Gallery.

## To England and France
Undiscouraged, George sailed to England to find a buyer. Clara waited at home until their second child was born. When she joined George overseas, she took with her one-year-old Elizabeth and the tiny baby, Clara.

In London, at first, the Gallery was a hit. Whenever groups of Indians visited from America, George included them in his program. Then drumbeats and war cries filled the hall—the first Wild West shows ever seen. The exhibit toured England for three years, but by then ticket sales had slowed to a trickle. And to George's disappointment, no one had offered to buy the Gallery.

By 1843, their fourth year in England, George and Clara had four children to support—Elizabeth, Clara, and new babies Victoria and George. They were struggling to pay their bills. For a fresh start—and a fresh audience—the Catlins moved to Paris, France.

## Sorrow and Loss
In Paris even the king of France praised the Indian Gallery, but still no buyer

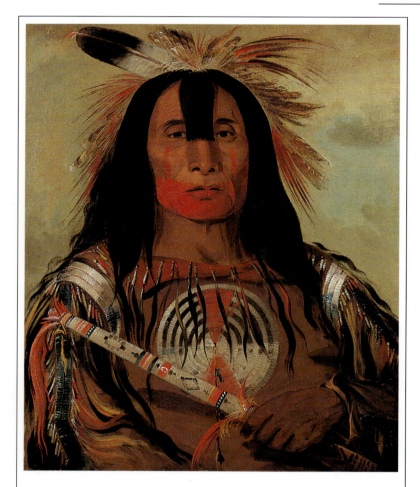

*A Blackfoot chief named Buffalo Bull's Back Fat*

could be found. Then, in that beautiful city, tragedy struck. Thirty-seven-year-old Clara got sick and died. Soon after, little George died, too. Heartbroken, George Catlin stayed in France, caring for his three daughters as best he could.

Still, he had hope for his art. In 1849 Congress voted on buying the Indian Gallery. In a strong speech, Senator Daniel Webster called Catlin's Indian paintings the most truthful "on the face of the earth." Even so, the collection was turned down. In 1852 Congress voted again on Catlin's work. But again George lost—by six votes.

He was now so poor that he went bankrupt. Clara's brother took the Catlin girls back to America to be raised. And the Indian Gallery was taken away by a rich American named Joseph Harrison because George owed him money. Harrison shipped the paintings and objects back to Philadelphia and piled them up in the basement of his boiler factory.

George was all alone now. In his fifties, he was growing deaf and his life's work was gone. Unwilling to return home a failure, he kept on wandering. He traveled for years in South America, first looking for gold, then painting the Indians of the South American jungles.

When his travels were over, George settled in Europe to write books and to paint. He could not rest while his beloved Gallery was hidden away in a basement. So, in a cold, rundown studio, he repainted many of the pictures in his lost collection, using old sketches to guide him.

*A young woman named Bending Willow*

## HOME AT LAST

In 1870, after thirty-one years away, George finally returned to America. He was seventy-four years old. The United States was a different country now. There were thirty-seven states, and wild places were harder to find. The railroad went from coast to coast. Buffalo were becoming scarce. And western Indians were losing the bitter fight to keep their land.

George painted almost to his last day—December 23, 1872. Sadly, he did not live to see the second part of his dream come true. But seven years later, it did. The Indian Gallery was cleaned up and donated to the Smithsonian Institution in Washington, D.C. It is still there today, part of our national treasure.

When George was young, he wrote, "I take incredible pleasure in roaming through nature's trackless wild." But he also did it for us. So that we could see what the West looked like when Indians ruled the Great Plains and the land was a sea of grass.

# Glossary

**American Revolution:** America's War of Independence from England.

**Andrew Jackson:** The seventh president of the United States, in office from 1829–1837.

**arrowhead:** The sharp, stone tip of an arrow.

**Big Muddy:** A nickname for the Missouri River.

**bluffs:** Steep cliffs, often on the banks of a river.

**cargo boat:** A boat used to carry goods on a river.

**Catlinite:** The red, claylike stone that Indians used to make pipes.

**Clark, William:** The explorer who traveled west with Meriwether Lewis in the Lewis and Clark Expedition of 1804–1806.

**Clinton, DeWitt:** The governor of New York State from 1817–1823 and 1825–1828.

**frontier:** The area where civilization borders on the wilderness.

**Great Plains:** The vast grasslands that stretch from the Missouri River to the Rocky Mountains.

**Great Spirit:** The main god of the North American Indians, sometimes called the Creator.

**legend:** A story handed down from one generation to another, often about a people's history.

**Lewis and Clark Expedition of 1804–1806:** The first exploration of the West by white men.

**Madison, Dolley:** The wife of James Madison, fourth president of the United States, in office from 1809–1817.

**medicine:** Special power that Indians believed was a gift from the Great Spirit.

**mustang:** A small, strong type of horse that was popular on the western plains.

**Native Americans:** The first inhabitants of America, usually called Indians.

**O-kee-pa:** The Mandan religious ceremony in which young men tested their bravery by self-torture.

**pemmican** (PEH-mih-kahn): Dried strips of buffalo meat, mixed with buffalo fat and berries.

**prairie:** Flat or hilly grasslands with few bushes or trees.

**regiment:** A large, organized group of soldiers.

**scalplocks:** Strips of hair from an enemy's scalp, used by Indians as decoration.

**smallpox:** A contagious disease that killed millions of people until it was wiped out by Edward Jenner's vaccine.

**steamboat:** A boat powered by steam, demonstrated by John Fitch in 1787 and Robert Fulton in 1807.

**tomahawk:** An axlike weapon used by Indians.

**the West:** The land west of the Mississippi River, unknown to most whites in the early 1800s.

# To Learn More About the Native Americans that George Catlin Painted

## Books (Fiction)

dePaola, Tomie. *The Legend of the Indian Paintbrush*. New York: Putnam, 1988.

Goble, Paul. *Buffalo Woman*. New York: Bradbury Press, 1984.

Goble, Paul. *The Gift of the Sacred Dog*. New York: Bradbury Press, 1980.

Goble, Paul. *The Girl Who Loved Wild Horses*. New York: Bradbury Press, 1978.

Yolen, Jane. *Sky Dogs*. San Diego: Harcourt Brace Jovanovich, 1990.

## Books (Nonfiction)

Fradin, Dennis B. *The Cheyennes*. Chicago: Children's Press, 1992.

Gorsline, Marie, and Douglas Gorsline. *North American Indians*. New York: Random House, 1977.

Greene, Carol. *Black Elk: A Man with a Vision*. Chicago: Children's Press, 1990.

Littlechild, George. *This Land Is My Land*. Emeryville, California: Children's Press, 1993.

Miller, Jay. *Native Americans*. Chicago: Children's Press, 1993.

Mooney, Martin J. *The Comanche Indians*. New York: Chelsea House, 1993.

*Off the Map: The Journals of Lewis and Clark*. ed. Peter and Connie Roop. New York: Walker, 1993.

Oppenheim, Joanne. *Black Hawk, Frontier Warrior*. Mahwah, New Jersey: Troll Associates, 1979.

Osinski, Alice. *The Sioux*. Chicago: Children's Press, 1992.

Wolfson, Evelyn. *Growing Up Indian*. New York: Walker, 1986.

## Museums

The American Museum of Natural History: Central Park West at 79th Street, New York, New York 10024.

The Field Museum of Natural History: Roosevelt Road at lake Shore Drive, Chicago, Illinois 60605.

The Gilcrease Museum: 1400 Gilcrease Museum Road, Tulsa, Oklahoma 74127-2100.

The National Museum of the American Indian (A Smithsonian Museum): One Bowling Green, New York, New York 10004.

National Museum of American Art, Smithsonian Institution: Eighth & G Streets NW, Washington, D.C. 20560.

The National Portrait Gallery, Smithsonian Institution: Eighth & F Streets NW, Washington, D.C. 20560.

## Videos

*Indians of North America.* (1990) The National Museum of the American Indian (A Smithsonian Museum), One Bowling Green, New York, New York 10004.

*Into the Circle.* (1994) The Gilcrease Museum, 1400 Gilcrease Museum Road, Tulsa, Oklahoma 74127-2100.

*Native American Life.* (1995) The Gilcrease Museum, 1400 Gilcrease Museum Road, Tulsa, Oklahoma 74127-2100.

## ABOUT THE AUTHOR

Nancy Plain is a writer whose special interests are history and art. She has written a biography of the painter Mary Cassatt, who was the only American to join the French Impressionist group. While studying Native American history at the University of Pennsylvania, Nancy read the letters of George Catlin for the first time. Writing a book about this brave and unusual artist has been a "wonderful armchair adventure," she says.

The author lives in New Jersey with her husband and three daughters. But if she could take a vacation in a time machine, she would like to travel the Missouri River in a steamboat to see what George Catlin saw in the 1830s.

# Index

Page numbers for illustrations are in boldface.

j921
CAT

Plain, Nancy

The man who painted
Indians

$21.36